894

Aluminium

If you look around you — at home, at school, in the streets — you will see hundreds of things made from aluminium. Yet we have been using this metal for only about 150 years. Before 1825, no one knew how to isolate it from the mineral alumina. Today, it is one of the world's most vital metals. It is used to make a huge assortment of products, from ships and aeroplanes to cans for fizzy drinks and foil for wrapping food. We use more aluminium than any other metal except steel.

This book looks at the reasons why aluminium has become so important to us. It traces the history of its discovery and explains how alumina is mined and processed. In clear, non-technical language, it describes the different methods of strengthening and shaping aluminium and discusses its many uses.

Jacqueline Dineen was an editor of educational books before becoming a freelance author. She now specializes in writing reference books for children.

Focus on
ALUMINIUM

Jacqueline Dineen

Focus on Resources series

Alternative Energy
Aluminium
Coal
Coffee
Copper
Cotton
Dairy Produce
Diamonds
Fruit
Gas
Glass
Gold
Grain
Iron and Steel
Nuclear Fuel

Oil
Paper
Plastics
Rice
Rubber
Salt
Seafood
Silver
Soya
Sugar
Tea
Timber
Vegetables
Water
Wool

Editor: Jillie Norrey

First published in 1988 by
Wayland (Publishers) Ltd
61 Western Road, Hove
East Sussex BN3 1JD, England

© Copyright 1988 Wayland (Publishers) Ltd

Phototypeset by Kalligraphics Ltd, Redhill, Surrey
Printed in Italy by G. Canale & C.S.p.A., Turin
Bound in the UK at the Bath Press, Avon

Cover *These racing bicycles have aluminium frames. They are light and very fast.*
Frontispiece *Aluminium is used to make a variety of products, from jet aircraft to these fizzy drink cans.*

British Library Cataloguing in Publication Data
Dineen, Jacqueline
    Focus on aluminium. – (Focus on resources).
    l. Aluminium – Juvenile literature
    I. Title
    669′.772   TN775

    ISBN 1–85210–319–1

Contents

1. A 'modern' metal

We use metal in so many ways that it is impossible to imagine life without it. There is nothing new about this: people have been working with metal for about 9,000 years. The first metals to be discovered were lumps of gold and copper. People began to experiment with them, and slowly they learned about the nature of metal. They discovered that it could be bent and hammered into shape. Copper is brittle, but heating, or 'annealing', was found to make it stronger and easier to shape.

Most metal was found in rock ores, and people learned how to heat the ore so that the metal melted and ran out of the rock. They found that melted metal could be cast into different shapes to make tools, utensils, ornaments and jewellery.

Gradually, more metals such as silver, lead, tin and iron were discovered. People learned

A pile of crumbly red ore can be turned into a bar of aluminium like this one.

how to make new metals, or 'alloys', by mixing two metals together. The first alloy was bronze, a mixture of copper and tin.

But nobody discovered aluminium. Why not?

The reason is that aluminium is not found as a pure metal. It exists in rocks and soil, but it is mixed with other elements, such as oxygen. It cannot be separated just by melting it away from its ore (a process called smelting). As time went by, scientists learned more about the properties of aluminium, but no one found a way to isolate the metal until 1825. That is why it is a 'modern' metal compared with copper, gold and the others.

Despite its late start, aluminium is now one of the world's most valuable metals. It is used more than any other metal except steel.

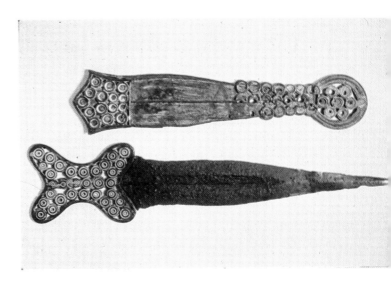

Above *Metals were used to make weapons like this Celtic sword and scabbard.*

Iron has been used for centuries. These fourteenth-century iron workers are shaping heated iron.

2. The history of aluminium

Aluminium is made from a mineral called alumina, or aluminium oxide. This is a compound of two elements, aluminium and oxygen, which are very difficult to separate. A British chemist and inventor, Sir Humphry Davy, made an unsuccessful attempt to isolate aluminium in 1807. In 1825, a Danish chemist, Hans Christian Oersted, managed to produce a few grains of metal by heating aluminium chloride with potassium. Unfortunately, potassium was very expensive, so it could not be used to produce the metal in large quantities. Thirty years later, Henri Sainte-Clair Deville, a French chemist, made the process slightly cheaper by using sodium instead of potassium.

Deville managed to interest the Emperor of France, Napoleon III, in the new metal. Napoleon supplied money for research so that Deville could improve his method. Small amounts of the metal were produced for sale, but it was more expensive than gold and was regarded as a great luxury.

The real breakthrough came in 1886. An American, Charles M. Hall, and a Frenchman, Paul Herault, working separately, discovered the electrolytic method of producing aluminium from aluminium oxide. (Electrolysis

Henri Sainte-Clair Deville managed to produce small amounts of aluminium for sale.

is a way of using electricity to split a chemical compound into its separate elements. This is the method that is used to produce aluminium today.) And two years later, a German named Karl Bayer found an efficient way of extracting aluminium oxide from bauxite (aluminium ore). Aluminium could now be produced at a price everyone could afford.

Manufacturers were very interested in the new metal, and aluminium companies soon began to spring up. In 1888, the Pittsburgh Reduction Company was set up in the USA, and six years later the British Aluminium Company began operating in Britain. Soon, all industrial countries were finding new and better ways of using this 'wonder' metal.

Above *Paul Herault (left) and Charles Hall found a new way to isolate aluminium.*

Furnaces for producing aluminium by the Herault method in late nineteenth-century France.

3. Why is aluminium so useful?

The lightness of aluminium makes it possible to build huge aircraft like this 747 jet.

People already had a wealth of metals to choose from, so why were they so excited about aluminium? Their reasons were much the same as those that make aluminium so popular today. Aluminium has several advantages over other metals.

Its biggest advantage is that it is very light. It is about three times lighter than steel, and four times lighter than lead. Aluminium is not very strong on its own, but it can be made as strong as steel if it is alloyed with other metals. Aluminium alloys are used where a combination of lightness and strength are needed, such as for ships and aeroplanes.

The fact that aluminium is closely linked with oxygen gives it another advantage. When aluminium comes into contact with the oxygen in the air around it, a very thin coating of aluminium oxide forms over the metal. This natural protective layer prevents corrosion, such as rust, which eats away at unprotected metal that is exposed to air or water.

Aluminium is non-toxic, which means that it can be used safely with food. This makes it a useful material for cooking utensils, for packaging such as foil containers, and for the machinery used to process food.

Copper is the best conductor of heat and electricity, but aluminium is almost as good. It is lighter and cheaper than copper, so it has many uses in the electrical industry.

But it is aluminium's lightness and resistance to corrosion that make it really valuable. The following chapter looks at these benefits in more detail.

The aluminium foil lids on these containers will not spoil the food inside.

4. How is aluminium used?

Aluminium was used in the building of the luxury liner, the Queen Elizabeth 2.

Aluminium's best feature is lightness combined with strength. Consider transport, for example. We have huge jumbo jets that carry hundreds of passengers at great speeds and heights. There are giant oil tankers and huge passenger liners. It would not be possible to build these very large craft without aluminium. A jumbo jet made of lead, or even steel, would never get off the ground! The storage tanks on some large tankers are made of aluminium, because heavy tanks would make the ships capsize. The world's largest passenger liner, the *Queen Elizabeth 2*, carries 2,000 passengers and 1,000 crew. It is an enormous ship, yet it is very light because aluminium and plastic were used to build the hull and make many of the fittings.

Iron and steel bridges are very strong, but the wind and rain soon corrode these metals. Aluminium alloys can be used to build graceful bridges that are strong enough to support traffic, and can resist the worst weather. Even when bridges are made of other metals, they are often sprayed with an aluminium coating to protect them from the weather.

Look around your own home and see how aluminium is used in smaller ways. Perhaps your house has aluminium window frames: these do not rust or rot. Maybe you have an aluminium ladder that is light enough to carry and store easily, yet strong enough to bear a person's weight. Perhaps you have a lightweight aluminium bicycle, built for speed. Look in the fridge or freezer and see how many foods are packed in aluminium foil. These are just some of the uses of aluminium.

Explorers tackling a climb in the Antarctic on lightweight, aluminium ladders.

5. Bauxite – the aluminium ore

The ruined village of Les Baux in France in 1864. Bauxite was first mined here in 1816.

The earth's crust contains a great deal of aluminium. It is even more abundant than iron, which is one of our most common metals. Aluminium is found in various soils and rocks, such as kaolin (china clay) and ordinary garden clay. This is probably how people first discovered its existence, when they used clays to make pottery.

However, no one has found an economical way of extracting aluminium from these sources. There is only one suitable aluminium ore, and that is bauxite. Bauxite is named after the village of Les Baux in France, where it was first mined in 1816.

Bauxite is not nearly as plentiful as iron ore, and between 4 and 6 tonnes are needed to produce 1 tonne of aluminium. Even so, there are about 25,000 million tonnes of bauxite in the earth, so there is enough to keep us going for some time to come.

The reddish-brown ore consists of 40 to 60 per cent alumina (aluminium oxide) mixed with other materials such as iron oxide, silicon oxide and water. It may be crumbly or like soft rock, depending on the part of the world it comes from.

In a bauxite mine mechanical excavators remove the ore. The soil is then replaced.

Geologists search for bauxite deposits until they find an area that contains enough bauxite to make it worth mining. The ore is mined by the opencast method. The topsoil is removed and the bauxite is scooped out by mechanical excavators. Then the topsoil is replaced. The bauxite is crushed, washed and dried before it is taken to the alumina plant, where the aluminium oxide is extracted.

6. Where is bauxite found?

Bauxite deposits have been discovered on every continent except Antarctica, but the types that contain the most alumina are found in the tropical and sub-tropical parts of the world. Australia has the largest deposits. The world's biggest bauxite mines, at Weipa in Queensland, contain nearly 3,000 million tonnes of ore and produce about 25 per cent of the world's supply. Jamaica, Guinea, Guyana and Brazil also have large deposits.

Many of the countries in the tropics are poor. They have large populations and there are few industries to support the people. The climate makes farming difficult, and people struggle to make a living as best they can. These countries rely on the export of natural resources, such as cash crops and minerals, to bring in money. Bauxite is one of these valuable minerals.

Aluminium is produced by large companies in the richer industrial countries such as the USA and Canada, who import bauxite or alumina. At first, the bauxite-producing countries were paid only low prices for the ore, while the aluminium companies grew rich. Naturally, the bauxite-producing countries found this unfair, so in 1974, some of them

This red lake in Jamaica has been formed from the wastes left over after bauxite processing.

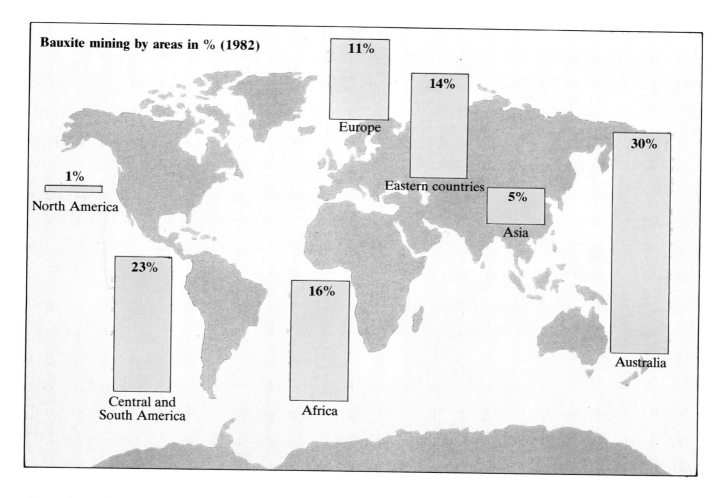

Bauxite mining by areas in % (1982)

11% Europe

14% Eastern countries

30% Australia

5% Asia

1% North America

23% Central and South America

16% Africa

Bauxite mining worldwide. Australia and Central and South America produce the most.

formed the International Bauxite Association. They set a minimum price for bauxite, and made sure that no one sold the ore cheaper.

The associaton succeeded in raising the price of bauxite, but has created a situation which the aluminium companies are not happy with. As bauxite is the only economical source of aluminium at the moment, there is no competition from other producers. This means that the bauxite-producing countries could force the price of bauxite up to unreasonable levels. That is why aluminium manufacturers are now trying to find other profitable sources of aluminium.

7. The aluminium companies

Aluminium is not manufactured by many separate companies, or even by a different company in each country. Production of most of the world's aluminium is controlled by just a few companies. The giant of them all is the Aluminium Company of America (Alcoa), which has more than fifty factories in different parts of the world. The other big name is Alcan Aluminium Ltd, which is based in Canada but has factories all over the world for refining alumina, producing aluminium, and making aluminium products.

The big companies constantly look for new bauxite deposits around the world. If they find worthwhile amounts, they arrange with that country to set up a new mine. Of course, the company has to pay the bauxite-producing country for the ore it mines.

The bauxite is either sent to a nearby alumina plant for refining, and the alumina is then shipped to aluminium factories in other countries, or it is exported in its raw state.

An aluminium factory in Queensland, Australia. The bauxite is refined before export.

Bauxite being loaded on to ships at Port Rhoades, Jamaica. It will be exported all over the world.

The largest exporter of alumina is Australia, which exports 6 million tonnes a year. It also exports large quantities of bauxite. However, Australia does not export all the bauxite and alumina it produces. Some of it is used to manufacture aluminium at plants in Australia, where nearly 500,000 tonnes of the metal are produced each year.

The main producers of aluminium are the USA, Canada, the USSR, Japan, West Germany and Norway. British Alcan Aluminium plc has factories for making aluminium and aluminium products in different parts of Britain. These producers, and other Western countries, are also the largest users of aluminium. More is being produced each year.

8. Producing alumina

Bauxite before processing. The ore has to be crushed and processed to remove unwanted materials.

When the bauxite has been mined, it is taken to an alumina plant. The unwanted parts of the ore have to be removed to leave the aluminium oxide, or alumina, from which the aluminium will be made.

Alumina is still produced by the method that Karl Bayer devised in 1888. First, the crushed and dried bauxite is mixed with liquid caustic soda and pumped into steam pressure tanks called 'digesters'. The alumina in the bauxite dissolves, leaving a mass of impurities known as red mud.

The red mud is removed by filtering the mixture under pressure. The alumina is now a clear brown liquid, which is pumped into tanks for the next stage of the process. Small amounts of a chemical compound called alumina trihydrate are added, and the mixture is agitated for a day and a half. The alumina trihydrate is known as a 'seed charge'. As the mixture cools, it causes the liquid alumina to separate into crystals of pure alumina trihydrate and caustic soda. The caustic soda is removed and re-used.

The alumina is now a damp, creamy substance. It is ready for the final stage of the process – calcination. First, the alumina is washed to remove any traces of caustic soda. Then it is fed into long rotary kilns which are slowly heated to a temperature of 1,000°C. This dries out all the moisture from the alumina, leaving a fine white powder.

The powdery alumina is cooled and stored in large silos. Then it is loaded on to cargo ships for its journey to the aluminium plant.

The damp alumina is dried out in kilns until it is a fine white powder.

9. Alumina to aluminium

The alumina arrives at the aluminium plant, ready for the final part of the process that will turn it into metal. This is the stage when the aluminium and oxygen are separated by electrolysis.

Everything on the earth is made up of basic chemical elements. Carbon, hydrogen and oxygen are elements, and there are about a hundred others. Elements cannot be broken down into simpler substances. When two or more elements are joined together, they form a chemical compound. Aluminium and oxygen together form the chemical compound known as alumina.

Electrolysis is a method of using electricity to divide chemical compounds into their individual elements. At the aluminium plant, it is carried out in a smelter. This consists of rows of

Pot lines in an aluminium smelter. The alumina is broken down by electricity in the pots.

Above *The ingots of aluminium are piled up and stored until they are needed.*

Below *The molten aluminium is poured into moulds and sets into ingots, or pigs.*

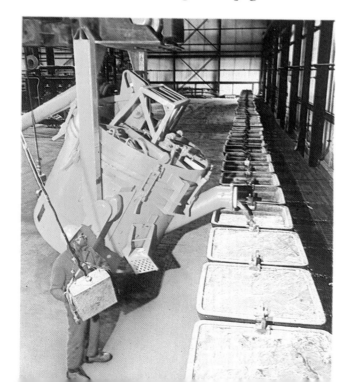

electrolytic cells known as 'pots'. Each pot is a steel box lined with carbon, with a carbon block suspended in it.

Firstly, the alumina is dissolved in molten cryolite, which is another aluminium mineral. The pots are filled with this mixture and then an electric current is passed between the carbon block and the carbon lining. The electricity breaks the alumina down into molten aluminium metal and oxygen.

The molten metal falls to the bottom of the pot. It is drawn off into a holding furnace, where it is checked to make sure that it is pure. The aluminium is then poured into rectangular moulds, where it cools and sets into blocks called ingots, or 'pigs'. This part of the process is called casting. The pigs are stored, ready to be made into aluminium products by the different methods described in the next chapters.

23

10. Aluminium alloys

Cars are made from strong aluminium alloys which protect passengers if there is an accident.

Aluminium is not a very strong metal. It is soft and ductile, which means that it can readily be bent and stretched into products such as wire. But pure aluminium dents easily and is not suitable for making things which need to bear any weight. However, if it is mixed with other minerals, it can be made very strong indeed. These mixtures are called alloys. For example, adding 5 per cent of silicon makes it three times stronger, and 5 per cent of copper makes it as strong as some types of steel. Manganese makes it stronger still.

Other minerals are added for different reasons. Aluminium and silicon is not as strong as aluminium and copper, but the molten metal flows more easily, so it can be cast into complicated shapes. Some minerals make aluminium more difficult to bend, or even more resistant to corrosion. The minerals usually mixed with aluminium are copper, silicon, manganese, magnesium, zinc, nickel and lithium. These are all types of metal, except silicon, which is a mineral found in the earth's crust.

How are these alloys used? To make door and window frames aluminium is alloyed with magnesium for strength and silicon to make it easier to shape. Manganese is added for items such as ladders and truck bodies. Copper, zinc, lithium, magnesium and nickel alloys are used for large structures which must be light and strong — cars, trains, ships, aircraft and spacecraft.

The pure aluminium pigs are melted again so that the new minerals can be added. The molten metal is then cast into ingots, which may be rectangular 'slabs', or log-shaped 'billets'.

Aluminium alloys are used to manufacture spacecraft like the US Space Shuttle.

11. Shaping the metal

There are two main ways of shaping aluminium and aluminium alloys. These are known as wrought forms and cast forms. Wrought forms are made by shaping the solid slabs or billets, while cast forms are made by pouring molten metal into moulds.

Wrought forms are shaped by rolling, extrusion, drawing or forging (see chapters 12 and 13). Cast forms are not as strong as wrought forms, but very intricate shapes, such as machinery parts, can be manufactured by this method. Casting is carried out in a foundry. Ingots of aluminium or alloy are melted in a furnace and poured into a shaped mould, where the metal hardens and sets. The principle is the same as making a jelly in a mould.

Molten metal is poured into these moulds and the lid is closed. The metal sets to the shape inside.

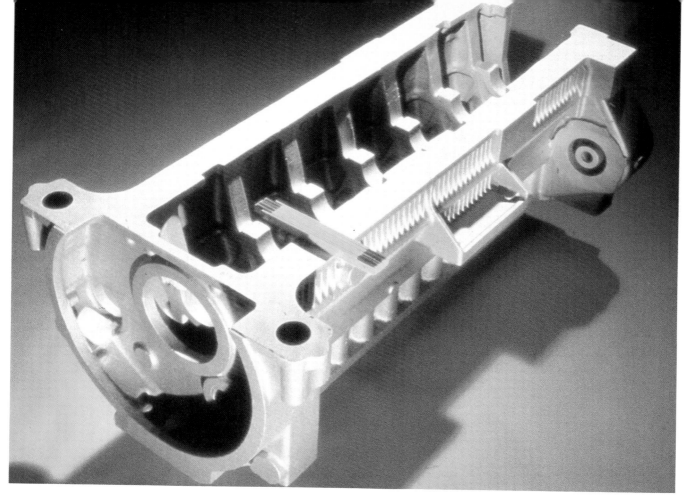

There are two methods of casting. One is sand casting, where the metal is poured into sand moulds. The other is pressure die casting. The molten metal is forced into metal moulds called dies under pressure, to make sure that it gets into every corner. The dies are then cooled with water. The metal must set, but not too quickly, so this part of the process is controlled very carefully. When they are hard, the castings are turned out of the moulds and cleaned.

Complicated shapes can be produced by casting. This is a part for a motor vehicle.

Pressure die casting is a quick and efficient method, which is used in many industries. The whole process is carried out by automatic machines that force the metal into the dies, cool it and turn the castings out at the end. Small castings can be made at a rate of one every three seconds.

12. Rolling

These slabs of aluminium are ready for hot rolling. Each ingot weighs 7 tonnes.

Wrought alloys are stronger than cast alloys, because the shaping of the metal toughens and hardens it. Processing is carefully controlled to give the metal the hardness and strength which is required.

The rolling method hardens aluminium at the same time as shaping it. Rectangular slabs of metal are rolled into thin lengths, just like rolling out pastry. There are two stages in the

rolling process – hot rolling and cold rolling.

In hot rolling, the ingot is heated until it is soft, but not molten. It is then passed back and forth between huge rollers that flatten it into a long, thin sheet. The metal is then given extra strength and hardness by rolling it when it has cooled down.

The process is carried out on huge rolling mills, which can flatten an ingot of 50 cm to a

Above *The ingot is passed between huge rollers which flatten it out to the required thickness.*

thickness of 2 cm in four minutes. The metal is then rolled to the required thickness, depending on whether it is being made into plate, sheet or foil. The name 'plate' is given to metal which is 6 mm thick or more. Sheet is between 6 mm and 0.15 mm thick. Anything thinner than this is called foil. A single ingot can produce up to 30 km of foil!

As it comes off the machine, the rolled metal is wound into huge coils, ready to be sent to the manufacturers. Plate is used for large structures such as ships and aircraft. Over 1,100 tonnes of aluminium alloy plate were used on the *Queen Elizabeth 2*. Sheet aluminium is used for building materials such as roofing, and to make many other products from household items like saucepans, to vans, buses and cars. Aluminium foil is a popular material for wrapping food.

Aluminium sheeting is used to make panels for buses like this one.

29

13. Extrusion, drawing and forging

Casting is a suitable method for making many intricately-shaped articles, but it cannot be used for producing long lengths of a particular shape, such as window or greenhouse frames. You would need a very strange mould for those! Articles of this type are produced by the extrusion method.

Imagine squeezing toothpaste out of a tube, and you get an idea of extrusion. Log-shaped billets are fed in at one end of the extrusion machine. At the other end is a die with the required shape cut in it. The aluminium is heated to soften it, and then forced through the machine at very high pressure. It comes out of the machine through the shaped hole in the die. It takes just a few seconds to produce up to 15 m of extruded aluminium. Even longer lengths could be made, but these would be difficult to handle.

Extrusion is not only used for making long lengths, however. It is also suitable for nuts, bolts, nails and other small articles. Hollow

In this picture, aircraft parts are being made by the extrusion method.

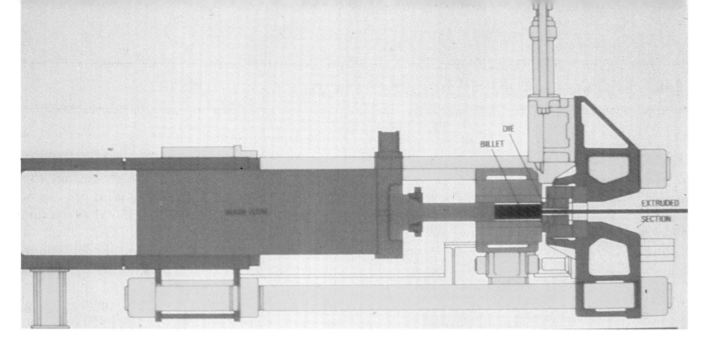

Above *The extrusion process. The aluminium is forced out through the narrow hole on the right.*

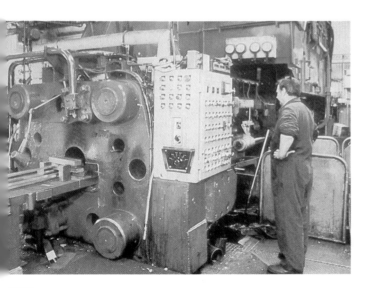

Long lengths of aluminium can be extruded on presses like this one.

pipes and tubes can be extruded, or made by another method called drawing. Here the metal is drawn, or pulled, through a machine that has holes of the required shape and size. Wire is made by this method. The metal is drawn through smaller and smaller holes until it is the right size.

Forging is one of the oldest metalworking methods. It goes back to the days when people heated metal and hammered it into shape. Nowadays, a hot ingot is pressed into shape by a massive forging press. The top of the press (the hammer) is shaped to press out the article against the bottom part (the anvil).

Forged metal is very strong and is used to make parts for aircraft, ships and military vehicles such as tanks.

31

14. Joining and finishing

Welding makes a strong join. Here, parts are being welded together at a car factory in the USA.

At this stage, there are many separate aluminium parts made by various methods. Many of these have to be joined to other aluminium parts, or to parts made of different materials. How is this done?

There are three methods of joining. One is to join the parts together with screws, bolts or rivets. Rivets are normally used for large constructions such as bridges and aircraft, because they are very strong.

Another way is by welding, which is used in shipbuilding and car manufacture. Great heat is applied to the parts to be joined, so that they melt and fuse together. Smaller parts can be joined by two other heat treatments: soldering or brazing.

The third method, bonding, can only be used for small, light articles. It literally means sticking the parts together with an adhesive.

Different finishes can now be applied to make the aluminium look more decorative. Polishing gives the metal a smoother, shinier surface. Saucepans are often finished in this way. Some articles are painted, either with a brush or by dipping the whole article into paint. Aluminium can also be plated with another metal, such as chromium or silver, to make a shiny article which is still very light.

Articles that are going to be painted, or that will be used outdoors, are often treated with a chemical finish to thicken the aluminium's oxide coating. This increases the metal's resistance to corrosion and is called anodizing.

Anodizing gives even greater protection against corrosion. The article is put into a bath of acid. An electric current is passed through the acid, and the reaction between the electricity and the chemicals produces a much thicker oxide coating. Anodized articles can be painted or given a bright finish.

These parts have been anodized and coloured. The finish will last and will not rust.

15. Manufacturing with aluminium

How many aluminium articles can you spot in your own home? How many can you see outside in the streets, in shops or in your school? You can probably pick out quite a lot, but some are not so easy to see. For example, aluminium is used to make small machine parts which are light yet strong. Knobs, dials, casings and trims may also be made of aluminium.

The building industry uses a great deal of aluminium. It has largely replaced materials such as wood, which rots and needs frequent repainting. As well as window and door frames, aluminium is made into roofing and wall cladding panels such as weatherboarding. Walls may be insulated with aluminium foil. Door handles, window catches, locks, shelving and

Aluminium window frames are easy to look after. They do not rust or need painting.

brackets may all be made of aluminium.

Next time you buy a fizzy drink, look at the lightweight can it comes in. What is it made of? Aluminium. If you have a take-away meal, it will probably be kept hot in aluminium foil containers. Bicycles used to be heavy and cumbersome. Now, some racing bikes could be picked up with one finger. The frame of a lightweight bike is made of aluminium tubing, and many of the other parts are aluminimum extrusions or

Aluminium railings stand up to all weathers and are strong as well.

die-castings.

Outside in the street, there are aluminium lampposts and traffic signs. Many crash barriers on roads, and railings on bridges and pavements are aluminium, because it can stand up to impact and does not need to be repainted as often as other metals.

16. Engineering with aluminium

It is amazing to think that a supersonic jet can be made from the same basic material as a fizzy drink can or cooking foil. Of course, only the strongest types of aluminium are used for making a supersonic jet. Duralumin is an aluminium-magnesium alloy, which is very strong indeed. It is used to make the frame, landing gear, engines and other parts of a supersonic jet – in fact, about 80 per cent of the aircraft is made from aluminium alloy.

Duralumin is also used to build ships, and not just huge liners like the *Queen Elizabeth 2*. Smaller vessels, built for speed, have to be light and strong too. Aluminium also resists corrosion by sea water.

It has been possible to make faster trains and cars by using duralumin and other alloys. The average car contains altogether about 50 kg of aluminium in the bodywork, the engine and other internal parts.

The aluminium hull of Virgin Atlantic Challenger II *was built for speed and strength.*

Aluminium is used to make the vast network of cables that bring us our electricity.

Aluminium plays an important part in other forms of engineering as well. Look at the giant electricity pylons that stride across the countryside. Between them are strung the cables that carry electricity into homes, offices and factories. These cables are made of aluminium wires, which are light and will not be damaged by bad weather. Aluminium is also used to make electric motors and parts for electronic and telephone equipment.

Chemical engineering plants often handle materials that are corrosive, and which have to be processed at very high or very low temperatures. So the heat-conducting and anti-corrosive properties of aluminium are very useful in the plant machinery and equipment.

Adorable
Inevitable → kaçınılmaz
ask out =
bring out, bring on
Rivet
Bonding
Knob, dials, casing, trims
Supersonic Jet
Duralumin → Al—Mg
landing gear   0/080 Aircraft

A wide range of cookware is made from aluminium because it is light and is safe to use with food.

Imagine that you are a fly on the wall in a modern family home. You are an unusual fly, because you are interested in finding out how many ways the family uses aluminium.

In the kitchen, you are likely to find aluminium frying pans and saucepans. Toasters and kettles are also often made of this versatile material. As members of the family use the cooker, the fridge and the freezer, and put the washing into the washing machine, you notice that these too have aluminum parts. Even the tops on the milk bottles are made from aluminium foil. If you continue your survey in other parts of the house, you may find that the

Above *One of the many uses for aluminium foil is the tops on milk bottles.*

Below *Look around your own kitchen and see how many things are made of aluminium.*

television is decorated with aluminium trim and the vacuum cleaner has aluminium parts.

Aluminium has many uses outdoors. Garden furniture can have tubular aluminium frames. Tents are often made with lightweight aluminium frames to support them. Sports gear increasingly makes use of aluminium — from tennis rackets to the reels of fishing rods. Food for a picnic is wrapped in aluminium foil to keep it cool and fresh, and thermos flasks are also made of aluminium.

18. Will aluminium run out?

You have seen how important aluminium is to us, and how many things are made from it. We are using more and more aluminium every year. But aluminium comes from bauxite, and bauxite is a mineral found in the earth's crust. Unlike plants, minerals do not grow again. It has taken millions of years for them to form and once they are gone, that is the end of them. At one time, people thought that we could never run out of the minerals contained in something so vast and deep as the earth's crust. Yet we can already see the day when we will run out of fuels such as coal and oil, and metals like gold, silver, copper and platinum. So will our supply of bauxite ever run out?

It is estimated that there are about 25,000 million tonnes of bauxite in the earth's crust. New supplies are discovered every year, so it is not very likely that we will run out of it in the near future. Even so, aluminium has become vital to our modern way of life, and we have to make the most of the supplies which the earth can provide.

Altogether, about 7 per cent of the earth's crust consists of aluminium, in bauxite and other rocks and soils. Experiments are being made in the USA to find economical ways of

This skyscraper shows how much aluminium has become a part of the modern world.

extracting alumina from clays such as kaolin. This would give us other sources of aluminium to fall back on, if bauxite supplies run low. It would also give bauxite some competition, and prevent the price from rising too high.

Another way of guarding against shortages in the future is to recycle the aluminium we already have.

We need aluminium, but we must also think of the effect on the countryside of mining. When a mine is finished with, new plants are grown in the soil. Soon the site of the mine will be invisible.

19. Recycling aluminium

Aluminium can be recycled by melting it down and recasting it into ingots. The metal may be scraps left from manufacturing, or it may be metal articles that have been used and thrown away, such as fizzy drinks cans and foil containers. A lot of recycling already goes on. In some places there are special bins in which to dispose of used drinks cans. Aluminium is very suitable for recycling because so many disposable items are made from it.

In Britain, about a quarter of the aluminium products manufactured each year are made from recycled metal. In the USA, there is even more recycling. Offices have collection points

In the USA, collection points for items which can be recycled are found in every big town.

This scrap aluminium has been collected for recycling. It will be made into new products.

where people can throw aluminium cans, and there are big recycling schemes. Even so, a lot of scrap aluminium is wasted.

The procedure for recycling aluminium is quite simple, and it is far cheaper than producing aluminium from bauxite, because less electricity is needed. In fact, recycling takes only 5 per cent of the electricity required for aluminium production. After collecting aluminium cans they are taken to an aluminium factory, where they are sorted and cleaned. Then they are put into a furnace and melted. The molten aluminium is cast into ingots in the same way as new aluminium. The metal is then used to make more drinks cans, which can also be collected and recycled, and so on. The same metal can be used again and again.

If you put your can in the dustbin, however, it will be thrown away with all the other household rubbish. That is one piece of aluminium wasted. Next time you buy a fizzy drink, think about how you dispose of the can.

Facts and Figures

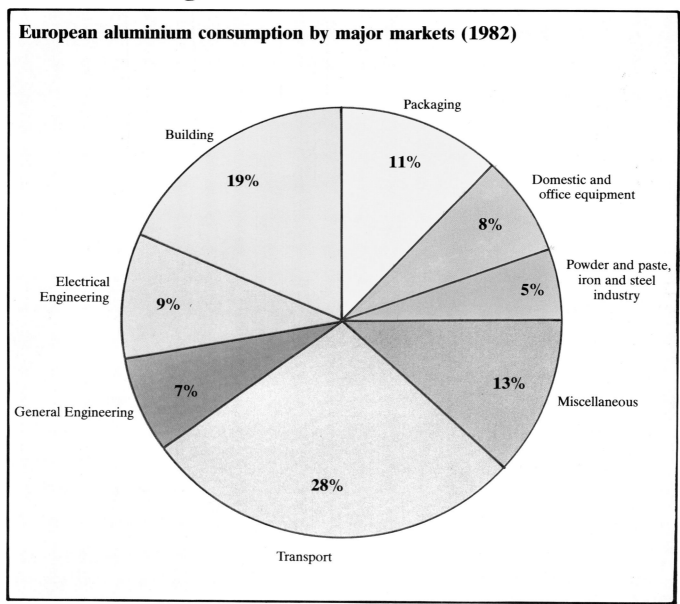

European aluminium consumption by major markets (1982)

Packaging 11%

Domestic and office equipment 8%

Powder and paste, iron and steel industry 5%

Miscellaneous 13%

Transport 28%

General Engineering 7%

Electrical Engineering 9%

Building 19%

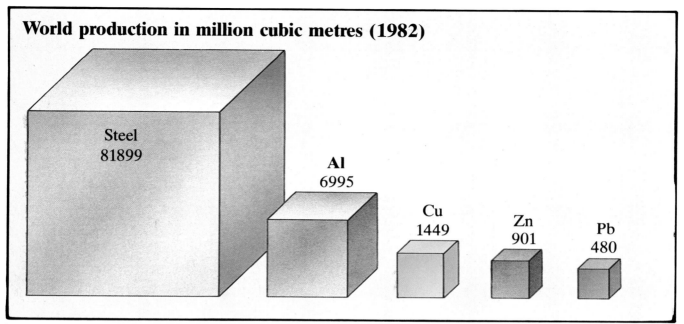

World production in million cubic metres (1982)

Steel
81899

Al
6995

Cu
1449

Zn
901

Pb
480

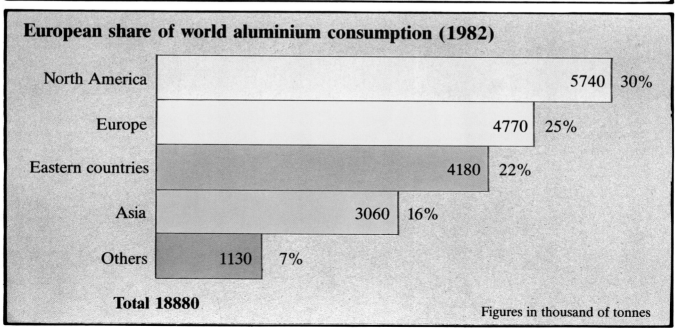

European share of world aluminium consumption (1982)

North America — 5740 — 30%

Europe — 4770 — 25%

Eastern countries — 4180 — 22%

Asia — 3060 — 16%

Others — 1130 — 7%

Total 18880

Figures in thousand of tonnes

Glossary

Alloy A mixture of two or more types of metal.

Alumina Aluminium oxide, a compound of aluminium and oxygen, which is the raw material for producing aluminium.

Annealing Heat treatment by which a metal is heated and allowed to cool slowly. This softens the metal, making it easier to work and less brittle.

Bauxite Aluminium ore — rocks or soil containing aluminium deposits.

Billet A log-shaped ingot of metal used for making articles by extrusion.

Brazing A method of joining metal by using molten brass to make the joint. It is suitable for joining items such as tubing.

Cash crop A crop grown for sale, rather than to feed the local population.

Conductor A material that can transfer heat or electricity.

Corrosion The eating away of metals by exposure to moisture or chemicals. Rust is a form of corrosion caused by moisture.

Earth's crust The outer layer of rock that surrounds the earth. It is over 20 km thick under land, and about 10 km thick under the oceans.

Elements The basic chemicals, or ingredients, from which everything on the earth is made. Carbon, hydrogen and oxygen are elements.

Geologist Someone who studies the earth's crust and the layers of rock beneath the surface.

Ingot Metal that has been hardened from a molten condition into a block or other shape that is suitable for further processing.

Mineral Any natural substance in the earth's crust that does not come from plants or animals. Rocks and metals are minerals.

Molten Melted into a liquid condition by great heat.

Ore Rock or soil containing deposits of a mineral that can be extracted. Aluminium ore is called bauxite.

Silo A large storage building.

Slab An ingot of metal shaped into a rectangular block. Slabs are always used for rolling.

Soldering A method of joining metal by using a molten alloy of lead, tin and antimony to make the joint. This alloy has a low melting temperature, but is only suitable for joining small articles, such as wires or pipes.

Sources of further information

If you would like to find out more about aluminium, please write to:

The Aluminium Federation
Broadway House
Calthorpe Road
Five Ways
Birmingham B15 1TN

British Alcan produce a booklet and other information for schools.
Their address is:

British Alcan Aluminium PLC
Chalfont Park
Gerrards Cross
SL9 0QB

Books to Read

LANGLEY, A. *Modern Metals* (Wayland, 1980)
KERROD, R. *Metals* (Macdonald Educational, 1981)
SIMONS, E. N. *The Story of Metals* (Pegasus, 1967)
AITCHISON, L. *The Story of Metals* (Ladybird, 1971)
KEEVIL, D. J. *Aluminium* (Wayland, 1980)

Picture acknowledgements

The author and publishers would like to thank the following for allowing their illustrations to be reproduced in this book: Mary Evans 14; The Hutchison Library 18, 23 (top); GeoScience Features 20, 41; Integrated Marketing Services 9 (top), 11, 13, 15, 21, 22, 25, 27, 28, 29 (both), 31 (both), 33, 35, 38, 39 (right), 43; Christine Osborne 34, 40; Photri 6, 23 (bottom), 26, 30, 42; Ann Ronan 8, 9 (bottom); Sporting Pictures *cover*; Topham Picture Library 32, 36; Malcolm Walker 17, 44–5; Wayland Picture Library 7, 39 (left); John Wright *frontispiece*, 19; ZEFA 10, 12, 16, 24, 37.

Index

,1944